MW01480020

The Book

of

Michael

By
Michael Robert Clark

I dedicate this book to my family and friends. My loving father and mother.

I want to thank God most of all, because without God I would not be able to do any of this.

About the Author

Michael Robert Clark was born and raised in McMinnville, Oregon, USA. For the last couple of years, he has been working on this book and writing poetry.

Michael is a firm believer in God, Christianity, and Catholicism. Although, he does not attend any church or services. His life revolves around the love for his family and friends, spirituality, and a passion for poetry and literature.

Preface

Over the years, I have been working on this book and writing poetry. I did what the Lord asked me to do. It was to write this book.

Contents

The Lord of Morea

One Ring, the Earth and sky.
One man will wear it.

Before Time Began

Shadows and humans hide.
Shadows deep inside.
Shadows are weak and die.
Before I doom speak, before I doom die.
Before time began,
In the shadows, we hide.

The Creatures Lie

In the shadows we run.
In the battle we hide.
In the Land of Morea, the creatures lie.
Before I speak and die.

Rest at Night

At the break of dawn, I will gather my men,
And we will leave to find our princess.
We will not stop until she has been found.
We will only rest at night.

In the Mirror

I can see her looking in the mirror.
She is in the distance.
I love my daughter.
She is a beautiful princess.
She is lying in the dirt.
He wants to marry my daughter.
Our beautiful princess.
He wants to become a prince.
I can see him looking in her mirror.
I could shoot him from this distance.
Isn't my daughter beautiful?
Isn't she a princess?
Doesn't she look fine?

Look Up at the Stars

Let me look at you my beautiful darling.
Let me gaze into your eyes
As we look up at the stars.
Let me whisper in your ear
And kiss you.

You May Die

Before I begin,
And our time is short.
The end you may die.

The Time Flies

Morea, I speak.
Morea, I die.
More I begin.
More the time flies.

John Has Wings

I twinkle my toes and I twinkle my nose.
John is laughing, and I am crying.
He has wings, and I do not.

Waiting to Fall

John likes high places.
He likes sitting on rooftops
Or high buildings.
He is just waiting to fall.

Life Is Beautiful

Life is beautiful
And far away,
And without you,
It is not the same.

Your life is beautiful,
And you live far away,
And without life
And no meaning,
And there is no truth,
And there is no justice,
And without life,
There is no meaning.

I am beautiful,
And I look every day,
And I look the same,
And you look different.

Without peace,
There is no justice,
And I will prevail.

Her Sweet Beauty

Her knights do not feed her.
They give her wealth.
They feed off her sweet beauty.

My Knights Need Help

Oh, my beautiful darling, where did you go?
  Do you need my help?
Did this dragon come to save you
  Or take you away from me?
Where did my knights go?
  When will they save you?
How long will it take?
  This knight said he would help.
This knight will take me to see my princess.

Turn Away

All those who wander are lost.
Those that journey, turn away.

The Fire in Which It Came

Taken out of the fiery pits of Hades.
Put back into Hell,
Or the fire that it came from,
Or from the fire in which it came.

Land of Lost

Land of Lost do not go back.
Land of Lost, turn away.

Eager to Fight

There is a battle over that mountain.
My men are eager to fight.
The sun is about to rise.
We will see what morning has to offer.
The battle is just getting started.
I am just getting warmed up.

Wayward Reach

We ride on the mountainside.
The Western Woods, I sleep;
Hunting Wayward Reach.
I claim this mountain.
I doom speak.

That Way

Fire Mountain is that way.
Be aware of dragons.

Known to Man

One more battle.
Creatures to be fought.
One more question,
And battle known to man.

Shadows Lie

In Morea, the Shadows lie.
Creatures have eyes.
They are demons.

Note to Man

One more story.
Battle to be wrote.
One more question.
Note to man.

Known to Man

Battles to be fought.
Creatures to be taught.
One more creature,
And battle known to man.

People Die

Battle and people die.
We challenge inside.
Battle and humans die.
Your weakness inside.

The Dragons Are West

My men are south,
The giants are north,
The fairies are east,
And the dragons are west.

Fear Me

Those who fear death, shall fear me.
  Those walls belong to me.
That castle is mine.
  I watched this castle grow.
That is my daughter.
  This is her bedroom.
Watch me lock it and seal it shut.
  Her bedroom door.

Go Unsaid

Let darkness descend upon light.
Let it take over the light
And dwell upon man.
Because no light shall go unspoken.
It shall not go unsaid.

My Knights Are Great

My knights are great.
They have swords.
They have a king and a queen.
There is a beautiful princess.

My Knights Are Men

My knights are men.
I keep them safe.
I will protect them.
I must defend my castle.

Defend Our Castle

Protect my knights and men.
Defend our castle.

Any Armor

A true king does not use a sword.
He does not wield any armor.

We Wait for Morning

The sun looks down over the mountain.
    Shining down on the valley.
Showing us the way home.
    This road leads us nowhere.

Where are we going? Are we going home?
    This road takes us back to the valley.
We must follow this one.
    We must scurry home.

We must follow this trail.
    This road does not take us home.
It leads us back to the valley.
    There is a shadow over the mountain.

This road is uncertain.
    We should not follow this trail.
We wait for morning to bid you farewell.
    The sun looks down over the valley.

It leaves us a trail.
    We do not know where we are going.
But we bid you farewell.
    This road takes us home.

Goodbye everyone and thank you for reading this story.
    I say goodbye and farewell.
We look down over the valley.
    The sun left us a trail.

Oh, Sir Robert

Oh, Sir Robert, I need you in battle.
To fight alongside me.
To serve and protect your kingdom.
To fight for what is right.

My Knights of Gale

Oh, sleep I have fallen on this grim passing tale.
Oh, sleep I have fallen and I dost thee well.
Farewell, my fallen, on this grim passing tale.
Farewell, my fallen, and I dost thee well.
I dost thee farewell, my knights of Gale.

Farewell, My Fallen

Oh, death to fire and men.
At dawn, they passage forth.
So, do thy knights of Gale.
I dost thee farewell, my fallen.

My Knights in Gale

Farewell, my knights in Gale.
The Lord you follow,
And the Lord you worship,
And I dost thee farewell.

The Unknown

I will travel down every road.
What wicked tales are in the unknown?

Tis Death

'Tis death, that slicks the slumber.
'Tis death, that slicks the arrow
And broadens the sword
And sleeps upon the arrow.

For a Ride

I will be right back.
I am going for a ride.
I will take my horse.

Her Knight Will Return

He fell with broken wings.
Guiding him from chaos.
Landing on his back.
He must face terrible foes.
They call this beast a dragon.
John will fight for his kingdom.
Ariel waits for her knight to return.

Goods They Have

Look at what they brought us.
All the goods they have to offer.

Sir Henry

Sir Henry, save me.
Defeat that is evil.
Protect that is strong.

Guns Are Being Fired

I can hear it.
It stirs across the land
And echoes across the valley.
Guns are being fired.

Nothing to Offer

You can see guns being fired.
You can hear it over the canyon,
And see it across the horizon.
My knights are ready to battle.
We wait for nightfall.
Dusk has nothing to offer.

Treachery Awaits

What hides in the shadows and sleeps in the dark?
What treachery awaits you?
What haunts down that road?

A Dark Hall

Behind those walls.
There is a gate.
Leading down to a dungeon.
Taking you to a dark hall.

There is an even darker story within that hall.
Within those walls lies your princess.
Taking you down a dark path.
Leading you to such ruins and finding fine jewelry.

Within this land you will find nothing.
But an even sadder story.
Staring into a dark room.
Looking up at the ceiling.

Looking down at your princess.
Finding her wrapped in chains.
Locked behind a door.
Not knowing where to run.

His Kingdom

A knight knows best.
He knows how to protect his kingdom.

By His King

A knight knows how to protect his kingdom.
A knight does not choose his own blade.
A man does not pick his sword.
It is chosen by his king.

Sir Knight Robert

Take this chalice to your lord.
   But do not let him drink from it.
For it could lead to his demise.
   If you fail to give him this cup.
Your life will be mine.

No man shall pick death.
   For it shall be your choosing.
For this shall be your last.
   Let him choose his own blade.

"Let death be his choosing.
   Let him pick his own sword.
What man would be without his own blade.
   Pick thy weapon wisely,"
Said Sir Knight Robert as he lays in a pool of death.

Sir Knight Robert has been defeated in battle.
   He has gained his knighthood.
He has shown courage and such bravery.
   He has shown valor.

The Fire You Came From

Back into the fire you came from.
For this shall be your last.
For I shall be your undoing.
For this shall be your doom.

One to Man

Nine rings under the Earth and sky.
Nine Mortal Men doomed to die.
Forbidden rings and power to man.
Fairies lay haste to the hands.
Forbidden powers and one to man.

Her Death Was Short

The hour has passed.
Her death was short.
Her passing was quick.

Name the Fear

Bound by God, name the fear.
Land has reached the sky.
Vanquish those demons.
Portray the land and sky.

Always New

Creatures of all the sky,
God has always known.
Flames across the land.
Shadows always know,
Flames are always new.

Oliver the Giant Slayer

Once upon a time,
There lived a princess in a castle.
One day she went missing.
No knight was there to save her.

One day a knight appeared.
Looking for our princess.
Not knowing where they took her.
Thinking where she had gone.

Searching for our princess.
Not knowing when to stop.
Going over mountains.
Reaching a nearby gate.

Going through mines.
Passing over mountains.
Reaching a nearby city.
Leading him to our princess.

Seeking haven.
Finding refuge with fairies.
Finding his princess.
He kisses her politely.

Once Upon a Time

Once upon a time,
There lived a beautiful princess.
In a castle not far from here.
One day that princess went missing.
Her knights were not there to save her.

Once Upon a Time

Once upon a time,
There lived a king and his kingdom.
He ruled throughout the castle,
And he searched throughout the land.

The Town of Hope

Oliver, our knight, continues to search for our princess.
He will not stop until she has been found.
He has come to the Town of Hope.
There lies a story about his princess.
He will continue to search from there.

One Day

One day Oliver will become a knight.
He will learn how to protect our kingdom.
He will also fight for our princess.

Have No Fear

Have no fear, princess.
Your knight is here to save you.
I have come to help.
We will flee together.

One Day

One day Olivia will become a beautiful princess,
And she will rule this land,
And a knight will come to save her,
And her kingdom.

Oliver, Our Prince

Oliver, our prince,
Has gone to save our princess,
And defeat the dragon.

Fear Not, Olivia

Fear not, Olivia.
One day this handsome prince will come to save you.
You will flee from this castle,
And those dreadful chains that you are wearing.

Knightly Deeds

Little blue fairy,
  Blow your horn once again.
To awaken the others
  And all good deeds.

Little blue fairy,
  Blow your horn once more.
To awaken the others
  And all good friends.

Little red fairy,
  Blow your horn once again.
To awaken the fairies,
  And all knightly deeds.

Little red fairy,
  Blow your horn once more.
To awaken the fairies
  And all knightly friends.

Little green fairy,
  Blow your horn once again.
To awaken the fountain,
  And all furry deeds.

Little green fairy,
  Blow your horn once more.
To awaken the fountain
  And all furry friends.

Trees Are Dark

Within this forest.
Hiding behind those trees.
There is evil waiting to come out.

Buried Deep

Deep within this mine.
Buried within these walls.
Around every corner.
There is a secret.

Mountains Are Dark

Behind that shadowy door.
Over that dark mountain.
Awaits your princess.

I Breathe Fire

I am a furnace of fire.
I am an unspeakable force.
I breathe fire.

A Cloud of Smoke

Trees are on fire; the village is burning.
A cloud of smoke up in the air.
We can see it over the horizon.
The fire keeps on burning.

Still Young

The night is still young.
  Look at our beautiful princess.
There is a knight here to save you.
  The king is fetching his horses.
His guards become men.
  They fight a terrible dragon.

Cave for Men

There is smoke over the mountains.
   There is a fire brewing.
There is a cave for men.
   There is a stable to keep your horses.
We stayed the night at the inn.

Hills Have Gold

There is a light that shines over the mountains.
  That light takes you home.
It shines over the valleys,
  Dark and desolate places.

Dark and Grey

Caverns are dark and grey.
They are filled with rocks and stones.
That is where miners keep their gold.

The Cavern Deep

Over the Misty Mountains
To the cavern deep.
Lies a treasure.

The Dam That Broke

Over the mountains to the sea.
Through the grassy fields.
To the dam that broke.

Treasure Gold

For the magic and story told.
The story is rich, and the story is old.
The magic is far and old.
The treasure is deep and buried gold.

Creature Old

In the kingdom,
In the sky,
In the castle below.
In the dungeon,
Dark and deep.
In the cavern,
Dark and old.
Lives a creature old.

Caverns Are Old

Dungeons are dark and caverns are old.
  They are filled with magic and gold.
We wait until the early break of day.
  To count our pail of enchanted gold.

The hills have spoken, trees have eyes.
  The sound of thunder and drums.
We need a light to show us the way.
  As we head through the dark.

A light shines over the mountain.
  Showing us the way.
Guiding us through the dark.
  Taking us back over the mountain.

The mighty dragon roars: we see his fire.
  We heed the dragon's tongue.
His mouth is roaring fire.
  We hear the beating of drums.

We wait for morning to turn as night arrives.
  As we look down over the mountain
And the dragon looks at us with his eyes.
  I fear what morning has to offer.

The mountain leaves us breathless.
  Cold without a fire.
The snow drops down on the hill.
  Leaving us stranded.

The sound of thunder and banging drums.
You can hear it over the mountain.
The dragon sits on top.
Waiting for his meal to arrive.

I must now end this story.
I must say goodbye.
This trail will not go unnoticed.
Our gold will not be left behind.

Your Knight Is Here

I have great news for you princess.
Your knight is here to rescue you.
He has come to defeat me.

Great News

Great news princess.
Your knight is here to save you.
He has come to take you away.

Here to Help

The king is here.
His knights have arrived.
They are here to help.

The King Is Angry

The king is angry.
Look at his face.
Have you seen his daughter?

You Will

You will become a knight
And save our princess.
You will cross new lands
And reach new heights.
You will soar over mountains.

Not Far from Here

Our knight continues his search.
He has reached new valleys.
He has gone far for our princess.
In a town not far from here.
Just west of this valley.
Right over that hill.
They speak of dragons and a cave.
Will this knight save our princess?
Who will kill those giants?

Sweet Misery

Death has nothing to offer.
Only pleasure and sweet misery.

A Hungry Knight

Seeking out his princess.
Finding her locked in a cell.
A dark scary dungeon.
A hungry monster awaits him.

I Will Not Stop

I will seek out my princess,
And find out where she is hiding.
I will pick every lock,
And look behind every door.
I will not stop looking for our princess.

Happily Ever After

One day I will return.
I have gone to save her.
We will live happily ever after.

Once Upon a Time

Once upon a time,
There was a king and a queen,
And a beautiful princess,
And they lived in a castle far away.

This Kingdom

I fear for our princess.
I dreamt that this day would come.
That I would have to take my knights,
And I would have to leave this kingdom.

Fee, Fi, Foe, and Fum

Fee, Fi, Foe, and Fum,
Cook me a bowl
And beat the drums.
Fimble-la-flam (fairies end.)

Beat My Drums

Pass me that boy, and beat the drums, Fim-fam-fum.
Bring me that girl, Be-bi-bum, and beat my drums.

No Giant

There is no giant on this earth.
Not a creature big or tall.
Not a creature little or small.
There is no giant.

Big and Tall

Not a giant,
Creature on this earth.
Giants are big and tall.

Lace My Shoes

Someone is knocking on my door.
I better lace my shoes and check.

From My Closet

Who is wearing my boots?
Someone stole them from my closet.

The Stirring Cries

The stirring cries, the sound echoes.
The sound of giants beating their drums.
They are searching for our princess.
The dragons sit on top of that hill.
They wait patiently for our princess.

You Look Lonely

You look lonely princess.
   Do you mind if I sit right here?
(Sit next to me dragon.
   Show me your teeth.
They are sharp like my sword.)

Boots You Are Wearing

What big brown boots you are wearing.
You should take them off your feet.
Stick them over there.

To Cut That

You are strong like an ox
And built like a fork.
You will need a knife to cut that.

Billy Will Help

Billy will help save our princess.
He must protect her.
He is not afraid of the other giants.

He Will Help

Billy is a giant.
He will help save Olivia.
He will protect her.

Thumb War

One, two, three, four,
Let's have a thumb war.
Let's battle with sticks.

Either One

Two sticks, bricks, needles, and twigs.
Bring me the blood of either one.

Hit Their Heads

Smash them up, hit them dead.
Smash this hammer on their heads.
Smash their fingers; hit them all.
Smash this hammer, hit their heads.

Set Me Free

One day dragon, I will defeat you.
A handsome prince will come.
That knight will set me free.

My Knight Will Come

Sleep now princess.
So, one day you will grow to become a beautiful princess.
One day you will rule this land,
And a handsome prince will come to save you,
And he will free you from those chains,
And lift you from that spell.

Tomorrow, my knight will come.
He will come to save me.
He will lift me from this spell,
And one day, I will become a beautiful queen.

No knight will come.
No one will save you princess.
You belong to me.

One day my knight will come.
He will come to save me.
He will free me from you.
He will take off these chains that I am wearing.

One Day Olivia

One day Olivia,
A handsome prince will come to save you.
He will free you from this land,
And lift you from that spell,
And he will take off those chains that you are wearing.

Beyond Belief

Beyond our forest and trees.
Beyond you and me.
Beyond belief.

He Reached the Top

John threw away his ladder
And climbed to the top of this tree,
And when John reached the top,
He fell.

I Reached the Top

I am picking apples from a tree.
I broke a limb.
This tree is getting taller.
I reached the top.

Terrible Beast

Giants have taken our princess
And conquered our lands.
Will there be a knight to save her?
What does this beast have to offer?
What is waiting for our princess?
What terrible beast awaits?

No Knight

Tossing and turning.
Waiting for our princess.
No knight has seen her.

Do You

Do you take this woman to be your wife?
Do you promise to be with her?
Do you dare stand before me?
Do you think you can defeat this giant?

Oh, Sweet Prince

Oh, sweet prince.
  Why have you not returned?
Why did you leave me?
  I am sitting here waiting for you.
Thinking about your return.
  I cannot live to wait another day.
Oh, how I love you so.
  I miss you clearly.

Leave Your Side

Oh, my beautiful princess.
I did not leave you.
I have been waiting for you here.
I would never leave your side.

One Day Oliver

One day Oliver, a young knight, will save Olivia.
He will take her away from this castle.
He will free her from this spell.

Fear Not

Fear not, my princess.
A handsome prince will come to save you.
He will free you from this castle.
He will take you away from this land.

Long Live the King

Long live my father and his dying queen.
May they watch over this land.
May their sons have daughters,
And may their children have children,
And may they rule this land.

Once Upon a Time

Once upon a time, there lived a dragon.
Not just any dragon.
She was not terrible or mean.

Ruler of the Land

Shadows of the land lay waste and cry.
One great king, the Earth and sky.
One great ruler of the land.
Portray the land and sky.
Land of Morea dies.

That Is Lost

Most men live by the sword.
Those who live and breathe.
Mainly men live by the cloth.
Therefore, I live in silence.
Those who wander are not lost.
Therefore, I live and breathe.
Therefore, I journey on this day.
To remember the land, far away.
Though I journey, far away.
To remember the land that is lost.

The Halls of Dark

The One Ring was forged by Elves.
It was taken out of its flames
And put back into the dark.
It was once used by man.
Then the dragons took it to protect their kingdom.
Now it lays on a stone in the Halls of Dark.
Where no man can touch it.

A Piece of the Dark

See the Ring of Fire.
Watch it glow.
Taking a piece of the dark.
Covering the land.

Standing By

I must challenge this knight and win.
I will battle him with my sword.
I will take out my bow
And shoot him.

I will grab my knife
And sword,
And I will cut off this giants' head,
And take him home.

I will rape all the women and children.
I will kill all the men.
I will take their cattle and feed them.
I will carry their saddles home.

There is a dragon
And I must defeat him.
I will unsheathe my sword.
This creature is not above me.

There is no gate to Heaven.
There is no Hell.
There is no earthly force or creature.
There is no God above me.

I am saying goodbye to all my fellow friends and warriors.
I am standing by.

To Be a Knight

A knight draws his sword when needed.
　He does not use it for anything else.
Serving his king and people.
　Saving the lives of men.
That is your virtue.
　That is what a true knight will become.
His king does not wield any armor.
　He does not beg for mercy.
That is what it means to be a knight.

A Sturdy Knight

A sturdy knight approaches the kingdom.
Wearing nothing but black armor
And riding a black stallion.
Riding into the kingdom.

A Strange Knight

A strange knight has appeared.
  Wearing nothing but black armor.
A dark horse he is riding.
  A heavy axe he carries.

A Valiant Knight

A valiant knight appears.
Showing off his sword.
Such a fine blade.
An elegant horseman.

A Shimmering Knight

Once a shimmering knight appeared.
Wearing nothing but black.
Riding a black saddle and horse.
Carrying the head of a dragon.

Left Alone

I will no longer sit in the dark or be left alone.
I will not be ignored.
My questions will be answered.
Is this what you are looking for?

God Is the Moon

God is the moon
And Lia is the stars.
She is beautiful.
I look at her every day.

Bright Like the Sun

God is the moon.
I can see Him every day.
He is bright like the sun.
I will ask Him to forgive me.

Long Live King Charles

Long live King Charles and his kingdom
And all the other kings and queens
And may they be reunited with their children
And may they live in harmony.

Leave at Dusk

Nor shall I see Death.
Nor shall he awaken my tomb.
I shall sit by the fire.
Waiting for morning to arrive.
Then I shall leave at dusk.
To await another morning.

Sleeps at Night

Death only sleeps at night.

Run Away

Land of Dragons,
You must turn back.

Land of Demons,
You must turn away.

Land of Giants,
Do not go back.

Land of Lost,
Run away.

Thank You, Filth

Put down that bridge.
Fill up my cup.
Saddle my horse.
Thank you, filth.

Down at the Sea

He walks up the mountain
And looks over the hill
And down at the sea.

Name the Sky

Burn the village
And land,
And watch them die.
Name the sky.

Evil Will Triumph

Evil will triumph,
And conquer our lands,
And take our pour cities.

Land Is on Fire

The land is on fire.
The village is burning.
There are soldiers fighting.

My Men Are Ready

His knights are getting ready.
I have gathered his horses.
They search for our princess.
The king's only daughter.

Magical Kingdom

In a kingdom not too far from here.
   In a castle over that hill.
Their lives our king in his magical kingdom,
   And so, lives his daughter,
And his beautiful queen,
   And there lies our prince,
And his magical story.

My Knight Is Here

My knight is here.
He has come to save me,
And take me away from this castle,
And those evil beasts that I used to call friends.

Fear Not

Fear not, my beautiful princess.
   I am here to save you.
I have come to rescue you.
   I will free you from this spell.
I will take off these chains,
   And we will escape this castle.

The Earth and Sky

One-man, the Earth and sky.
He was old when he died.
He walks past the land.
He set fire to the sky.

The Earth Cries

Flame by flame the Earth cries.
One by one the Earth dies.

Rule the Sky

Four for the Elven Lords,
And nine are doomed to die.
One Ring will rule the sky,
One Ring will bring them all,
And One Ring will bind them,
And the darkness will find them.
In the Land of Morea, the Shadows lie.

One Ring to rule them all,
One Ring to bind them,
And the darkness will find them.
Bring them all and find me.

The Ring Under the Sky

Nine rings to rule them all,
Nine rings to bind them.
Name the ring under the sky
And fill the land with gold.

One Ring

Nine for the Dwarf-lords, seven for humankind,
Three for the Elves, and four for the Orcs.
In the Land of Morea, shadows lay waste and cry.
To portray the land, the Earth and sky.
One Ring to rule them all, One Ring to find them,
One Ring to bring them all, and the darkness will bind them.
In the Land of Morea, shadows lay waste and cry.

Keys to the Kingdom

Here is thy key.
You will need it to open this door.

Golden Armor

My king, I oppose.
His lordship has grown.
His white knights and golden armor.

I Pray That God

I pray that my knights are in Heaven.
I hope the Lord is keeping them strong.
I pray that God is there with them.
I pray that He is watching over them.

To Become a Queen

There is a great king and queen.
They have knights and men.
They have a beautiful daughter.
One day to become a queen.

Knights Do Not

Knights do not dwell in camp.
They live in the city.
Feeding off the rich,
And stealing their horses.

That Fiend

Your knight is here.
Your prince has come to save you.
I will free you from this wretch.
That fiend.

A Great Knight

With my sword and shield, I will protect my king.
I will swear my allegiance to him.
I will become an even greater knight,
And I will protect my king,
And I will defend my kingdom.

If Needed

Do not cower in front of me.
Stand behind me if needed.

I Have

I have a sword,
A shield, and a bow.

I Am Yours

God, please watch over me.
Give me the power and strength to become a knight,
And one day I will become a king.
I am yours.

I Count the Days

I remember you
And this place.
This place I call home.
I count the days.

He Will Run

Fire always burns.
People fight young.
We die, everyone.
Battle is to be won.

In our prayers, we have won.
In this battle, we have done.

We will win! We have won!
Hear this song, I have heard.

In this battle, we have won.
Children sing, I have heard.

Crying people fear.
Dry your tears.
People run.

Dying people fear.
Battle always burns.
Fire we have seen.
Demons even speak.

We win, we have won!
Battle is to be won.
We will cheer.
We won.

Evil demons and lord.
Battle is to be heard.

Battle he will run.
He has had.

Fear of You

Win a battle we have done.
Win a war; we have won.
Fear of dying. Yes, we have.
Fear of you. Yes, we heard.

Humans Fear

Dry your eyes
And cry your tears.
We had fun
And we did play.
Children cry,
And people die.
Humans cry,
And humans fear.

Even Run

Fear of shadows even might.
Fear of queens, even lord.
Fear of dragons, even sword.
Fear of soldiers, even run.

Become a Knight

Grab your sword
And grace it with your hands
And become a knight.

We Will Win

He is beautiful,
And he has knights,
And I must save them.

My knights are beautiful,
And they have swords
And a king.

I am a king
And this is my castle,
And these are my knights.

I am beautiful
And I have knights.
They defend me.

I am a knight,
And this is my sword.
I will show you.

I have knights,
And a sword,
And we will win.

Become a Knight

Pick up your sword.
Take this bow and arrow.
Grab your shield.
Become a knight and win.

Dear God

Dear God,
Please send me an angel.
One that will do me no harm.
One that will protect me.

Up There with You

I pray that God is up there with you.
I pray that He is keeping you strong.
I pray that I was there with you.
But now is not my time.

That Is Evil

I must protect my people.
Defend them from harm.
All that is evil.

I Am Not Alone

Christ, I am not alone.
You are here with me.
You have shown me the way.
Through trees and forest.
You are my defense against him.
You are broad like my sword.
I have shown you, my courage.

Mighty Like Thor

God is powerful.
He is mighty like Thor.
There is Odin.

And Win

Pick thy blade and arrow.
Choose thy sword and win.

God Be with You

May God be with you
And watch over you forever,
And let God be the one to judge you.
Even through battle,
And may God give you peace.
Amen!

Tales From the Dark

Ghouls and ghosts across the land.
Creatures come out, the nights and days.
Name the ghoul and godly fear.
On a moonless night, your children play.

Grown Tired

All the children are locked in their rooms.
Their parents have put them away.
They have all grown tired.

Bedbug's Bite

Tuck in your children and tell them goodnight.
Do not let the bedbug's bite.

Toys in My Attic

This story is wicked.
The voices in my head told me to write this.
There are demons and they like to play.
There are children and they are having fun.
There are demons in my closet.
There are monsters underneath my bed.
There are toys in my attic.

Off to Sleep

My children are off to sleep.
I tucked them away.
I told them goodnight.

The Town of Merry Day

In the Town of Merry Day,
All the children are tucked away.
They are all safe and sound.
Their parents put them to bed.

In the Attic

My wife is downstairs in the basement.
Folding her dirty laundry.
I am cleaning the kitchen sink.
I heard a noise in the attic.
I will have to find out what it is.

Rest for a While

The voice tells me to stop.
But I keep on going.
I should rest for a while.
Then continue my journey.

Keep On Going

The voice is getting louder.
I can hear it inside my head.
The voice tells me to stop.
I should not stop.
I must keep on going.

Stomp Your Feet

The sound of feet pounding.
You can hear it down the stairs.
Two children stomping their feet.
I thought I told you to go to bed!
My kids rushed upstairs
And jumped into bed.

215

The Moon Rises

They sleep until the sun goes down.
They wake up when the moon rises.

The Town of Yesterday

In the Town of Yesterday,
We wait until morning to break the day.
We only face obstacles.
When the day has been said and done.
The morning has just begun.

I Intend

This light is unbearable.
I intend to destroy it.

Take Out His Chest

Carve out his pumpkin.
Take out his chest.
Stick a blade through his heart.

Conjuring Evil

I summon a soul.
A spirit from the Underworld.
I call one into this room.
I demand you to open this door.
I do not seek your power, only judgment.
I want you to guide me through this room.

Mine to Keep

Pick any card from this deck.
Let no one else see it.
For it your choosing
And mine to keep.

She Is Quiet

My wife is upstairs.
She is checking on the baby.
I can see her crying.
I will hold her until she is quiet.

Evil Presence

There is an evil presence in this house.
I can feel it.
It is getting stronger.

I Am Still

He is looking at me.
I can see him clearly.
He is moving softly.
Question, am I still?

They Come Out at Night

They come out at night.
Right after sundown.
When the moon looks at the city
And everyone is asleep.

I Will

I will take thy children home.
I will eat their skin and bones.

Children and Toys

Children and toys, laughter, and noise.
  We are having lots of fun
And building lots of toys.
  For all the fun children.
That brought us lots of noise.

Need Not Fright

Watch me, goblins, on this night.
My children need not fright.
My goblins in the night.

I Mean Trash

Spooky ghouls and goblins.
Take out the garbage.
I mean trash.

In My Attic

There is a monster in my closest.
There is a monster underneath my bed.
There is a demon in my attic.

In Your Closet

Take your shoes and socks off.
Stick them in your closet.
They will be underneath your bed.

A Beautiful Angel

A beautiful angel appears in the sky.
Descending upon everyone else.
Everyone looks with remark and such beauty.
Staring at her wings.

The Lord Jesus Christ

Shadows of the land and sky.
One ruler and king,
The Lord Jesus Christ.
Jesus is our Lord,
And God is our Savior.

God Is My Blade

Michael casted out Satan.
Sending Hades back to Hell.
Kneeling before God.
Showing Him his blade.
God draws out His sword.
Michael stands.
Michael walks away.
Showing his back to God.

The Last Prayer

I pray to God and Jesus.
I pray that they listen.
I hope the world is doing ok.
God created this food.
God thank you for that.
God healed my wounds.
I pray that Jesus is coming.
I wait for Him here.

Broken Wings

I feel broken without my wings.
Looking at the world.
I wish I could do better.
Holding my cross in my hands.
Praying that Jesus is watching over me.

Christ You Are the Answer

Christ you are the answer to all my problems.
  You are what I asked for.
You have done so much for me.
  You have given me hope.
You have given me a place to live.

God Will Listen

Let us pray.
Bow your heads.
Close your eyes.
God will listen.

I Believe

I believe that God is in Heaven.
  That He is up there waiting for us,
And when the time is right.
  We will all go to see Him.

Thank You, God

Thank you, God, for watching over us on this day.
Thank you for this food and beverage.
Thank you, God, for healing Abraham's son Isaac.
Thank you for letting us live.
In your name, amen.

I Pray That

I pray that Jesus is watching over me.
I pray that He is near.
I pray that he is weak when the Lord is around.
I pray that God will lead us to Him.

A New Place

I work for the Lord.
He has given me a new home.
A new place to do business.

I Will Ask God

I will ask God, to see if it is ok to use His name.
So, I do not slander His name
And commit a crime.

A Man of Faith

God is awesome
And He is great.
I am a man of Christ
And a man of faith.

Speak His Name

Speak His name,
And He will rise above us,
And He will live.

Now Is Not My Time

I wrote this poem for my grandma.
I pray that she is in Heaven.

I ask that you are in Heaven.
I hope the Lord keeps you strong.
I wish I was there with you.
But now is not my time.

Vows to Keep

The forest is lovely, dark, and deep.
The forest is dark, and lovely.
The forest is dark and deep.
I have vows to keep.

Miles before I sleep.
The Lord I seek.

The Forest Deep

I have miles to go.
I have miles before I sleep.
The Lord I seek.
He is in this forest.
He is buried deep.

I Do Not

He is not God.
I do not worship him.
I do not preserve.

God Knows His Kingdom

God knows His kingdom.
Showing it to the world.
Looking down at everybody.
God smiles at everyone.
You should also be happy.

I

That is what this demon said to me.
It said it wants my soul.
It wants to be a part of me.
I will not let it in.

II

I found this demon hiding in my attic.
It was hiding in this box.
So, I sent it back to the shadows.
That is where it came from.

III

I will see what this demon has to offer.
I reckon it wants my soul.

IV

What devil wrote this book?
What does evil have to offer?

V

A demon lurks in the shadows.
Hiding, waiting to come out.
It does not know when to stop.
Eating your soul.

VI

This demon is real.
It wants to take ahold of you.
It wants to control you.
It wants your soul.

VII

Evil is a part of us,
And it is inside us all,
And it will take control.

VIII

The Devil is real,
And he is a part of us,
And he is inside us all.

IX

I am a doll,
And this is my house,
And that is my toy,
And those are my children.

X

I will not enter this room.
I will not perish or die.
There is no sign.

XI

He feeds on the innocent
And prowls in the dark.
When the Lord is not around.

XII

He who enters this room.
Will perish and die.

XIII

Merry Christmas to you, my child.
(Thank you, father.)
I am sorry, you are dead.
I buried you.

XIV

You glimmer in the shadows,
And you hide in the dark.
The sky is yellow.
It is burning bright.

XV

There is a voice inside my head.
That voice is growing and getting louder.
That demon is real.
Those children want me to play.

XVI

This demon,
This doll
Speaks to me.
It moves
And listens,
This monster.

XVII

I call out Satan.
I call out all evil.

XVIII

You will die of a terrible death.
You will only have one child.
You will see your child grow.
You will rest among the stars.
You will see your father in Heaven.

XIX

Go back into the pit you came from.
Crawl back into darkness.
That furnace you call Hell.
I will lock you behind this door.

XX

Speak God, not Satan.

XXI

Death to all that follow.

XXII

My brother is James.
His king is John.
Michael is my brother.
His sister is Mary.
He has a brother named Luke.

Demon Brought

One demon brought me a child.
   The other one handed me this gift.
He brought me a sword.
   To slay the rest of them.

Evil Record

There is a demon hiding.
Lurking in the shadows.
Waiting for you to sleep.
Then it pops out.

I Cast You Out

I cast you out of Heaven,
Back into Hell.
Where you belong.

No More

No more demons on this earth.
No more Satan.

You Must

You must cast this demon away.
You must let this spirit out.
You must not let it take ahold of you.

No Evil

Show no fear, bring no evil.

God Is Not Satan

Let this cross be my light.
Let it guide me through the dark.
Let it beknown that God is not Satan.

Forgive Me, Father

Forgive me, father,
For the crimes and sins, I have committed,
And for the crimes that I will commit.
Please forgive me for what I have done.
(I forgive you, my child.)

Stay Focused

The Lord calls out your name.
He wants your pain.
He seeks your suffering.
He wants you to stay focused.

I Looked Your Way

You looked beautiful today.
You walked around,
You went downtown.
I looked your way.

Dear God

God will forgive you, my child.
Let us pray to Him.
Let us ask Him for forgiveness.

Dear God,
Please watch over us on this day.
I ask you to heal us.
I would like you to forgive us for our sins.

My Sweet Angel

Oh, my darling, my sweet angel.
My beautiful daughter.
My Annabelle.
How I love you.

My Sweet Annabelle

Oh, my sweet Annabelle.
How I love you.
How I miss you, my child.
Where did you go?
Where did your father take you?
Where did he leave you?
My sweet child.
I love you so much.

The Lord Watches Over You

Remember my child,
That the Lord is watching over you.
That He waits for you in Heaven,
And there you will be with Him.

Take Me to God

Take me to God, so I can sit beside Him.
There I will triumph.

Hand in Favor

Accompany me with the Lord.
Take His hand in favor.

Read the Bible

I welcome you all on this day.
Let us turn to our books.
Let us read our bibles.

I Found God

I am in the forest.
I am looking for Jesus.
Instead, I found God.

God Found You

The truth is that God found you.
   Sitting in the dirt;
Lying in some rubble;
   Digging through trash cans;
Taking what you like.

Please Michael

Please Michael, help me!
Save me from the Devil.
Save my soul from him.
Do not let him steal that from me.

Take Me Away

Take me away from this wretched place.
This evil world.

Demons Wander

I said no, and I mean, stop!
Her spirit belongs to me.
That soul is mine.
Let her talk.

Heal Me, Father

Heal me, father, for I have sinned.
I have done unrighteous things.

He Has to Offer

You have done well my child.
You have asked the Lord for His blessings
And you have seen what He has to offer.
Now go and be unseen,
And do not let anyone follow.

Speak Now

Speak now or forever, hold your peace.
Stick out your tongue.
So, that I may heal your body,
And grant you wisdom.
So, that you can see more clearly.

Forgive Me, Father

Forgive me, father, for I have sinned.
My last confession was just a couple weeks ago.
(You are forgiven, my child.
Do not use the Lord's name in vain again.)

I

God said that Jesus would come.
That He would deliver us to Him.
There you will find peace.

II

God told me of this day.
He said that He would come.
That we would find His son Jesus.

III

God told Moses to not linger or fall behind.

IV

God said to Moses,
"Take my cup,
And fill it to the rim,
And drink from it."

V

Thou shall praise God,
And not worship the Devil.

VI

Thou shall not turn on thy king.
Thou shall respect thy men.
Thou shall not attempt to do murder.
Thou shall not use the Lord's name in vain.
Thou shall obey the law.

VII

God was not crucified on the cross.
It was His son Jesus.

VIII

Go back to thy home.
You do not talk to me.
You do not speak.
I squander.

IX

Obey thy father and mother,
And do what they ask.

X

I want to be like John.
 I want to sit next to Jesus.
I want to drink with the Lord,
 And fill up His cup.

XI

I will not dye my hair.
I will not use makeup.
For it is an ugly color.

I will not change or look different.
I will not exceed my limits.
I will not drink or abuse alcohol.
For it could kill you.

I will do you no harm.
I will look good in the presence of the Lord.
I will not be frowned upon.
I will not carry a gun.
For it could be dangerous.

I will be treated fairly and alike.
I will not be judged by the color of my skin.
I will look no different.
It does not matter if I am Black or white.

I will read the Bible.
For it is true,
And there is no other.
For He is God.

XII

David is king.
He defeated Goliath.
He did not use a sword.

XIII

Thou shall praise the Lord
And worship Him,
And Him alone.

XIV

For God is awesome
And there is no other.
For God is my king,
And I am His servant.

XV

He who believes in God.
Will live an eternal life.

XVI

God would not punish you.
Abraham did not kill his son Isaac.

XVII

David is my power.
He is my strength.
I have no weakness.

XVIII

One day He will join us.
We will all gather around.

XIX

When I return,
I will take you to see Him.

XX

For the Lord is my shepherd
And I am His sheep.
He will lead me to a better place.
For I am His son,
And that is His daughter.

XXI

God told Isaac of his father.
That his death would be murder.

XXII

It was God that created this earth and wrote the Bible.
It was Him that saved Moses and rescued his people.

XXIII

Here lies Adam, before Eve.
There is God and Michael.

XXIV

God forbid Adam and Eve.
He told them to not eat this fruit.
That it would certainly kill them.

XXV

God brought Him from the dirt.
He took His ashes.

XXVI

No one knows what happened to Moses.
But God knows he saved his people.

XXVII

God said to Abraham,
"Watch over your son Isaac.
Look after him closely."

XXVIII

God spoke to Isaac.
He told him of his father.

XXIX

God gave David the power and strength to defeat Goliath.

XXX

Go forth and be after him.
But realize.

XXXI

God created man.
Then woman and child.

XXXII

Thou shall not steal, cheat, or lie.
Thou shall not ridicule my face.
Thou shall not look any different.

XXXIII

God said to Adam and Eve,
"That they could eat all that is His.
But not that of mine."

XXXIV

God spoke to me and said:
"Walk through this alley
And you will find comfort.
You will sleep at this inn."

XXXV

Speak nothing but the truth
And the whole truth only.

XXXVI

Christ was a man.

XXXVII

Jesus Christ was born.
God's only child.
To find His followers,
And share His wisdom.

XXXVIII

God said to Abraham,
"Take your son Isaac to the Land of Moriah.
Where he will be sacrificed and burnt."

XXXIX

Thou shall obey the Lord,
And do what He asks of you.

XL

The truth is that I needed healing.
That is why I turned to God.
Christ has healed me.

XLI

I.   Thou shall read the Bible.
II.   Thou shall obey all laws.
III.   Thou shall not judge one another.
IV.   Thou shall respect me for who I am.
V.   Thou shall not cheat on thy spouse.
VI.   Thou shall worship the Lord.
VII.   Thou shall not talk about the Devil.
VIII.   Do not commit a sin.
IX.   Thou shall not disobey thy father and thy mother.
X.   Thou shall not be misguided.

XLII

He is the son, not the Father.

XLIII

With the Lord by my side, I can do anything.
That is how David defeated Goliath.

XLIV

With new strength came power.
David felt confident.

XLV

"Walk with me, said the Lord,
I will take you to see God.
With Him you will feel strong.
There you will sit beside Him."

XLVI

Go with the Lord and be by His side.

XLVII

Take His heed; seek His warning.

XLVIII

God was once a child.
He walked among the living.
He now walks among the stars.

XLIX

Christ rose from His grave.
People were amazed.

L

Jesus rose from the dead
And was brought back to the living,
And then an angel appeared.
Not knowing that it was Him.

LI

Blessed is His name.
His chapel is holy.
So, are God's people.

LII

God is watching over you.
He is waiting for you in Heaven.

His Name Only

Speak His name and His name only.

He Is Victorious

David is now king.
He is now our leader.
He is victorious.

Let This

Let this ring guide you.
Let this spirit lead you.

May You Know

May you know God.
May you not seek such evil.
May it not take a part of your life.

Touch His Face

When I look up,
I can see God's grace.
But I cannot touch His face.

For His Glory

I will go back in time to save Jesus.
I will stand in His presence.
I will fight for His glory.

Christ Is Upon You

Christ is upon you, my child.
He is upon everyone else.
I look at you with grief.
Because you have deceived me.

I Believe

I believe in God.
I believe that His words are true.
I believe that there is no other before Him.
I believe that God created this earth.
I believe that God gave you a choice.

I Believe

I believe in the Lord Jesus Christ.
I believe that God brought Him to this earth to die for our sins.
I believe that God is not Jesus.

Christ Appeared

Christ appeared to me just for a while,
And within that time, we spoke.
I spoke to Him of my losses.
How badly I was broken.

We Spoke

Within that time, we spoke.
That hour of grieving.

Let Us Pray

Let us pray and worship God.
Let us welcome Him on this day.
Let us all bow our heads and praise Jesus.
Let us sing Hallelujah.

I Believe

I believe in the Lord Jesus Christ.
I believe that He died for our sins.
I believe God lifted Him up.

I Believe

I believe that God is my creator.
I believe that He created us for a reason.
I believe that we all have a purpose.

God Does Exist

I believe that God does exist.
I believe that the Lord is my Savior.
I believe that there is only one God
And Christ will take us to see Him.

You Are Forgiven

Please, forgive me, father,
For what I am about to do,
Or the things I have done.
(You are forgiven, my child.)

God's Glory

May God grant you, His power.
You seek His wisdom.
Find God's glory.

I Ask of Thee

Oh, heavenly Father,
I speak thy name.
I ask of thee.

I do not speak bad about thee.
Only good things.

Christ Is with Him

Oh, brothers and sisters that are dead.
I pray that you are in Heaven,
And I pray that God is with you,
And that Christ is with Him.

Leave Your Side

He will always be there for you.
Even when you are alone or feel left out.
God will be there for you.
He will never leave your side.

Seek His Glory

May God be with you and your children.
May He grant them a better life.
May you find His wisdom,
And seek His glory.

Prayer to Saint John

Saint John, I seek your wisdom and guidance.
   I offer you, my blessings.
I would like to know more about God.
   I would like you to teach me.
I have read your stories.
   You know so much about Christ.
You were one of His followers.

Pick It Up

This cross is upside down.
I will turn it around.
I will pick it up.

Sincerely Yours

I work for God
And the people.
Under one nation
And one roof.

I work for Sam.
I work for you
And the people.
I work for Him.

You are beautiful
And I am great.
You are Cupid
And this is his cross.

You are his bolt and arrow.
I am his lighting.
You are wicked
And I am strong.

You are intriguing,
You are beautiful,
You are sincere,
And you are kind.

Sincerely yours.

"I walked a crooked mile.
I had a crooked style."

The Sea Is Beautiful

This ship is beautiful.
When do we sail?
(We will sail at dawn.
Leave no one behind.)
I, I captain.
(Argh maties.)

God Was There

God was there when I needed Him the most.
God was there when I felt left out.
God was there when I needed healing.
When I had my ups and downs.

I Believe

I believe that Christ died for our sins.
That God brought Him to this earth,
Not just to die for our sins.
But to become a leader.

Puff, the Magic Dragon

Puff, the Magic Dragon,
In a land far and free.
A land for you and me.
He lives in harmony.

Puff, the Magic Dragon,
He lives by the sea.
In a land of harmony.
He shines so vividly.

Stars for you and me.
Clouds in the sky,
Puff in the wind,
And smoke in the breeze.

The Lord Watches Over Me

When the day is finally over
And the night arrives
And all the children are sound to sleep.
I pray that the Lord watches over me.

Show No Signs

Show no signs of the Devil.
Do let him control you
Or take any part in your life.
May that be your blessing.

Christ Appeared

Christ appeared to me as an angel
Brought from Heaven.
He took me to this chapel.
This place of offering.
So, that I may worship Him.

A Gift from God

Oh, Christ was born.
Her child was a blessing.
A gift from God.

Oh, Mother Mary

Oh, Mother Mary, I seek your wisdom.
  I pray that your Child is with us.
I symbolize your glory.
  You have shown us your mercy.
I have seen evil disappear.

I pray that Christ is near.
  I hope that this suits you.
A symbol of my faith.
  I wear it often.
A crown that symbolizes your glory.

Follow the Lord

"Come with me," said the Lord,
"Follow me to this place."
I will follow the Lord,
And see where He takes me.

St. Michael

St. Michael, I call you into battle.
Lucifer has appeared.

Prayer to Saint Joseph

Saint Joseph, please watch over me in Heaven.
Be my protection from the Devil.
Become my knight in battle.
Be my host in victory.
Lead me down the right path.

St. Michael

St. Michael, I call unto you in Heaven.
I ask nothing of you.
I would just like to see your glory.

Dear God

Dear God, watch over me in Heaven.
Protect me from Lucifer.
Be my knight in victory.
Become my host in battle.
Lead me down a straight path.

He Fell Over

Gabriel is this tree.
I think I will climb him.
I hope I do not fall.
There is someone standing up there.
I can see.

I climbed up.
He pushed me down.
I climbed right back up.
He fell over.

God was standing up there.
He pushed me down.
I climbed up.
He fell.

He knocked me over.
I picked myself back up.
I climbed back up.
God fell over.

I died and went to Heaven,
And I came back.
You will not pick me up.
You will not push me over.
I am this tree.

Back Demon

In the name of the law,
Back demon!
Go back to thy place.
Go back to thy home.

Mine Is Ezekiel

A language I udder hear or speak.
My brother is Michael.
His king is James.
Mine is Ezekiel.

Translate This Tongue

I cannot translate this tongue.
It is in another language.
It is in Hebrew.

He Was Me

I was God
And He was me.
We are two.
We are now three.
God and the Devil.

Valley of the New

As I walk,
I go to this place.
As I walk to the valley.
I do believe in God.

Thank You, God

Thank you, God,
For healing me on this day.
As I go, I leave this place.
In the Lord, Jesus Christ, amen.

God, the Father

God, the father,
The Spirit, and Earth.

Thank You, God

Thank you, God, for not hurting Isaac.
Thank you for letting him live.

He Will Not Fall

Peter can fly; he will not fall.

Protect the People

Spirit of Jesus.
Speak Dante,
And speak Satan.
Uphold the law,
And keep the peace,
And protect the people.

I Am Your School

I am your pastor and priest.
I am your school.

I Could Not

He kissed me.
I smiled and laughed.
I could not stop blushing.

The Air I Breathe

Beautiful, the air I breathe.
The morning laughs.
Beautiful, I am free.
The air you breathe.
I am lonesome.
I am lonely too.
I am here with you.

You Are Not

You are not innocent my child.
Your heart is cruel.
You are sustained.

Prayer to Saint Michael

Archangel Michael, please help!
Save me from Lucifer.
He has come to take my soul.
I would rather offer my soul to you.
Then become a part of him.

God So Loved the World

God so loved the world.
He gave you, His son.
His everlasting child.
A forgiving son.
A pastor and priest.
To hold and forget.

Anna Elisabeth Michel

From this ash, she awoke.
From this garden.
I remember her breath when she was dying.
Her breath stank.

I remember the pastor and priest
That performed this exorcism.
I will forgive them and this child.
Her death is mourned, and she will be grieved.

Take all the innocent women
And children and bury them alive.
Stick a cross over their heads,
And watch them squirm and squeamish.

I will drown you in a pool
And eat your carcass.
I will eat your liver and spleen.
I will drown you in a river.

Emily is sad and she is crying.
She is slowly dying.
She mourns.

The true nature of Emily Rose.
Her death was mourned.
Her parents and family will remember her.
And she will live on in history.

I Call God

I call God!
To release the demon
And cast you out.
To the demon
And demonic prayer.
To Christ, your brother,
And the holy affair.
A vengeful death is sweet.

Speak His Name

Speak His name for He will listen.
Do not let him hear you.
For God will undue his treachery
And shine upon everyone else.

I Serve God

I serve God.
I am not a slave.
I will not be plunged.

Have One Another

Someone to have and to hold.
To cherish and honor.
To love and forget.
To have one another.

Left You Break

For you I serve.
I pick God.
Path, I pick.
Left you take.
I take right.
Left you break.

His Kingdom Waits

Christ said that God was watching over us.
He waits for us in Heaven.
His kingdom is in the clouds.
Christ you must follow.
His kingdom waits.

Thank You, God

Thank you, God, for showing me the way.
For lending out your ears.
For creating a wonderful world.
For all those years.

Christ Appeared

Christ appeared before me when I was alone.
 He knew that I needed healing.
Christ answered my prayers.
 My thoughts needed healing.
Christ saved me.

God's Holy Kingdom

The Lord has blessed you, my child.
  He has washed away your sins.
He has seen your face.
  He showed you, His glory.
You are now part of this church.
  God's holy kingdom.

Seen His Face

Do not doubt the Lord.
    You have not yet seen His face.
You have seen His glory.
    Look at God's world.
Look at what He created for us.

Christ You Know

Christ you know you are amazing.
You are my Lord and Savior.

I Want to Live

I woke up this morning feeling good about myself.
I think I will sleep,
And wake up in the morning
And live.

Thank You, God

Thank you, God, for watching over me.
For healing me when I was sick.
Thank you for healing my wounds.
For healing my scars.

Praise Jesus

I will stand up and look at the Lord.
I will lift my hands above Him.
I will praise Jesus.

The One You Want

I am the one you want
And look for.
The one you love
And hate.

My Child Too

Brother James.
Our kingdom Michael.
My child too.
His kingdom is God's.

I Have Sinned

Forgive me, father,
For I have sinned.
I have done a terrible thing.
(I forgive you, child.)

The Things I Will Do

Please, forgive me, father,
For what I have done,
And the things I will do.
(I will not judge you, my child.)

I Repent

Forgive me, father,
I have sinned.
I repent.

Dear God

Dear God in Heaven,
Please watch over me and my children.
Please protect us both from harm.
Let us bear witness.

St. Michael

St. Michael,
Protect me in battle.
From the wickedness
And snares of the Devil.

He Is up There

God looks down at you
And everyone else.
He is up there in His kingdom.
Waiting for you to come.

Please Michael

Please Michael,
Protect me from the Devil.
Do not become a slave.
Do not wear that pendant or cross.
That is not God.

I will protect you from the Devil.
I will not wear that chain around my neck.
I am not a slave.
I will only serve God.

I believe in God.
I will live an eternal life.
I will wear this cross.
It fits around my neck.

St. Michael,
Protect me from Lucifer.
Do not be his slave.
Do not wear that pendant around your neck.
That is not a cross.

A Recipe

1 glass,
1 shot of liquor,
1 sip of wine,
1 lemon, 1 lime,
1 cold cider,
And 2 cups of tea.

Made in the USA
Las Vegas, NV
26 October 2023

79603458R00252